Foreword

Bishops of London have lived at Fulham for well over 1,000 years and the present 132nd Bishop is delighted and privileged to remain in touch with all the recent developments. I am an enthusiastic supporter of the work of the Trust and the remarkable transformation it has brought about.

In previous centuries bishops may well have been regarded as 'Princes of the Church' but I very much regret the official who changed the Fulham House of the early 18th century into the Fulham Palace of the 19th century. A similar development happened at Lambeth. I am glad that bishops have returned to their much more primitive role ▯▯▯▯▯▯ Christ. It mea▯▯▯▯ a much simple▯▯▯▯ has become a▯▯▯▯▯▯▯▯▯▯▯.

However, had history been different I should have enjoyed living at Fulham. Nonetheless, bishops always had a residence in the heart of London and as the first Bishop to live in the City since the early 17th century, I feel that I have revived one ancient tradition while with regret bidding adieu to another one.

The Rt Revd and Rt Hon Richard Chartres KCVO DD FSA, Bishop of London

Bottom right: Fulham Palace from the Thames, 1795, showing the south and east fronts.

CONTENTS

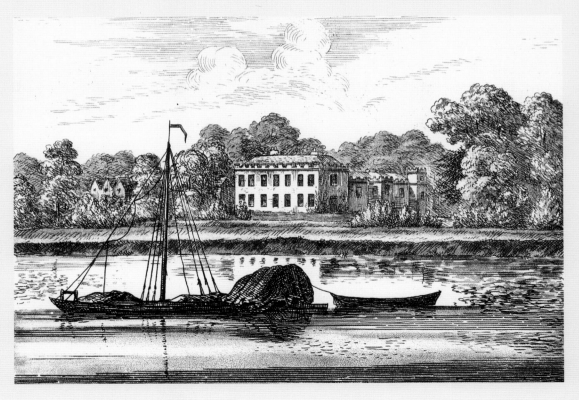

Introduction

Fulham Palace, just four miles from Hyde Park Corner, hidden inland from the Thames and the busy Putney Bridge, occupies an ancient site of national importance. A manor house for over a hundred successive Bishops of London, the largest domestic moated site in England, scene of royal banquets for Queen Elizabeth I, a famous botanical garden, and a fascinating mixture of architectural styles, Fulham Palace tells an intriguing story.

Fulham Manor, one of the most ancient in Britain, was acquired by Waldhere, Bishop of London, in about 700 AD. Robert Stopford, who retired in 1973, over twelve hundred years later, was the last bishop to live at Fulham. Bishops' homes became known as palaces from the 1700s because bishops were considered "princes of the church". The Bishops of London used Fulham as their country residence until 1920 when it became their principal home. Before 1939, the whole of the building (70 rooms) was lived in by one bishop, his family and a full staff of servants. When in residence, the Bishop would run the Diocese from the Palace, receive candidates for ordination and entertain dignitaries and members of the church from all over the world. In 1975, after a campaign by the local community, the Palace and gardens were leased by the Church Commissioners to Hammersmith and Fulham Council for one hundred years. Since 2011 the Fulham Palace Trust, a registered charity, has run the site.

Fulham Palace was listed as a Grade One building in 1954. The moat and the thirty-six acres it encloses were designated a Scheduled Ancient Monument in 1976. The estate is now thirteen acres, and the historic garden is listed by English Heritage. The present building can prove confusing to the first time visitor. It is easiest to think of Fulham Palace as a "Hampton Court in miniature", with a Tudor building first, followed by Georgian rebuilding to the rear in the classical tradition. It formed part of the ribbon of great houses that developed along the Thames to the west of the overcrowded City.

The grounds were opened to the public in 1974. The site was used for events, but there was limited access to the building. The first Fulham Palace Trust was formed in 1990 and the Museum opened in 1992. However it was not until the advent of the Heritage Lottery Fund that major capital works were possible. Phase One of the Restoration Project (2005-6) benefitted from a grant of £3.56m (with partnership funding from Hammersmith and Fulham Council and the Trust), resulting in a restored

east courtyard with a café, gallery, improved museum and hospitality facility. A further £6.48m from the HLF for Phase Two (2010-12) enabled the restoration of the vinery in the walled garden, improvements to nearby Bishop's Park, and the conversion of the stables into the Jessie Mylne Education Centre.

The Moat

Looking down from the bridge at the main entrance gates visitors can see part of the moat. It is the longest domestic moat in England and encloses the 36 acre Palace site forming the boundary of the current Scheduled Monument. Its origin is still a matter of debate. The first dated reference was in 1392 to a "magna fossa" or great ditch. The depth of the water varied from 1.2 to 2.1m. Sluices could be opened at high tide to fill the moat with river water from the Thames or at low tide to empty it. In 2009 archaeologists discovered the main sluice still in situ near the west corner of the moat. It can be seen from Bishop's Park and the outlet in the river wall is visible from the foreshore.

After complaints that the moat was "insanitary", Bishop Winnington-Ingram proposed to infill it. The moat was also dangerous: in 1883 two seven year old boys were found drowned. Despite a public outcry, the Bishop went ahead and the moat was filled with builders' debris from 1921-4. This section of the moat and bridge were excavated in 2011 when archaeologists found remains of an earlier timber bridge dating back to 1249-85 together with pottery dated 1270-1350. Finds from the 1920s infilling included glass and stoneware bottles and an enamel sign. The present bridge is late-medieval, refaced in about 1815.

Left: Section from an 1831 estate plan showing the moat, and inlets from the river.

Right: Archaeologists recording the timbers which have since been re-buried.

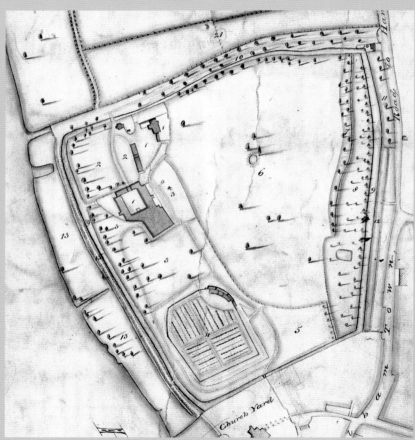

Main entrance to West Courtyard

Visitors now enter from Bishop's Avenue through the impressive wooden gates (replaced in 2012). The Bishop would have travelled by river, landing at the "Bishop's Stairs" to the south of the Palace until c.1800. Once roads had improved, a servant was needed to open the gates. The Porter's Lodge, built of brick faced with Roman cement (now returned to its original pink hue) was built c.1815 in the fashionable Gothick taste for Bishop Howley, whose arms can be seen over the porch. According to local antiquarian Thomas Faulkner it was designed by Lady Howley. The limestone gate piers were probably built at the same time.

Left: Watercolour by H. W Burgess 1833.

Right: Watercolour by J.G c.1880, showing moat, sluice and paddock.

The Coachman's Lodge opposite (1893) was designed by William Butterfield to replace the lodge built by Bishop Jackson in 1872 at the northern end of Bishop's Avenue. The latter was acquired by the local vestry for the park keeper when Bishop's Park was opened. All three lodges are now private residences.

Continuing along the main path, the lawn to the right was called the Paddock. Until the river wall was built in 1893 this area was frequently flooded at high tide. Excavations by the Fulham Archaeological Rescue Group here from 1975-6 produced evidence of a double-ditched enclosure, believed to be the site of the twelfth century Manor House. Do not go into the courtyard but turn left outside the archway. On the left are the stables, all that remains of the home farm.

An 1869 inventory includes 12 chickens, 13 pigeons, 5 pigs, 7 cows, and 2 carthorses in the farm buildings at Fulham Palace.

Alongside the barn was the Monk's Walk, immortalised in a poem on Bishop Bonner's ghost by Hannah More. The stables were rebuilt in 1873 after a fire in which a favourite pony died. When Bishop Winnington-Ingram acquired a car around 1905 some of the stables were converted to

garages. John Burley, the coachman, became the Bishop's chauffeur, his son John taking over in the 1920s.

Turning right you can see a line of chimneys which delineate the edge of the Tudor building. The north front is composed of three different periods of Georgian architecture. Immediately ahead is an extension added in 1814. Beyond is a two storey Palladian addition designed for Bishop Sherlock c.1753 by an unknown architect. Archaeological excavations in 1986 and 2005 revealed foundations of medieval buildings to the north of the existing ones.

The seven pointed windows are all that remain of the Gothick chapel designed for Bishop Terrick by the architect Stiff Leadbetter. Three new façades in the fashionable Strawberry Hill taste were added in 1764-66, unified by crenellations and towers. Bishop Howley remodelled the Palace once again in 1814-1818. His wife's cousin, Samuel Pepys Cockerell, removed the superficial Gothick details, added an extra storey and brought forward the east façade to create an unbroken rather severe elevation.

Bishops' Tree

Previous page

Top right: The Tithe Barn c.1899.

Bottom left: "Fulham House as it stood before the alterations in 1814" Watercolour by unknown artist c.1790.

On the north lawn is the Bishops' Tree, formed from a Cedar of Lebanon felled in 2006. The sculptures were carved by Andrew Frost (mainly with a chainsaw) in 2007 and donated to the Palace by Dolores Moorhouse in memory of her husband, Peter. Some of the lettering and carvings relate to the family.

The nearby oak bench shows Bishop Compton (1675-1713), who was a keen plant collector. He imported plants from all over the known world including the *Magnolia virginiana* from America which was grown for the first time in Europe at Fulham. The grounds became famous and visitors such as John Evelyn, the diarist, came to see the exotic plants and trees.

Bishop Bonner is at the foot of the tree. A Catholic, he was Bishop of London twice in the 16th century and during the reign of Queen Mary I is said to have tortured Protestant prisoners at the Palace. At the top of the tree is Bishop Porteus (1787-1809). He followed the fashion for the picturesque in the grounds where he made a rustic grotto and planted a grove of trees with a "narrow retired walk behind, called the Nun's Walk".

Victorian bishops took an interest in the surviving rare trees and added to the collection. Amongst them was Bishop Creighton (1897-1901), shown climbing up the tree. He was an important historian and is commemorated in the east window of the Chapel.

East façade onwards

Now turn right onto the main lawn. A clear expanse of lawn was needed for the famous garden parties; in the 1890s Mrs Creighton entertained almost 4,000 guests at a time. At the back of the lawn is the entrance to the walled garden.

Walk alongside the building and turn right. Here is Leadbetter's south façade, clad in wisteria, where the keen eyed visitor can spot a modern staircase inside the former garden entrance. Safe access is now possible to the upper floors which are rented out as offices. A Victorian corridor incorporating earlier brickwork links the main building to the Tait Chapel (1866-67), built in a Tudor revival style. Turn right by the chapel; the south wall was built onto an existing garden wall. Behind this wall is a Tudor extension, bearing the weathered coat of arms of Bishop Fitzjames (1506-22). Two of the three sets of bargeboards (decorative timbers protecting the brickwork) are 17th century. This may have been the principal entrance to the Palace but by 1763 it had become a service area. The ghosts of Bishops Bonner and Laud are said to reside here.

Continuing along to the right, the path through the woodland (reinstated in 2006) leads back to the west courtyard and main entrance. To the left glimpses may be had of the bank of the moat, and beyond that Bishop's Park.

Bottom left: Postcard c.1910 showing the old cork oak.
Top right: The Tudor extension to the south front.
Bottom right: Leadbetter's south façade and the Tait Chapel.

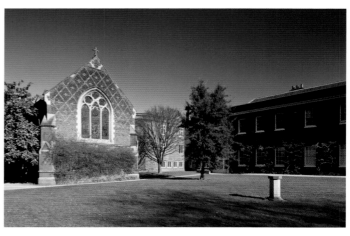

The West Courtyard

The west courtyard is the most reproduced view of the Palace. Seen through ancient oak gates the scene has not changed substantially over the centuries. The walls (c.1500) are built of red brick, with diamond patterns popular in the early Tudor period. The tower, similar to that of the Old Palace, Hatfield, was an early addition. The buildings served as storage with accommodation above; the 1647 inventory includes a bakehouse, spicery, coal house and apple lofts. Bishop Blomfield rebuilt the south wall; his coat of arms, dated 1853, is over the central doorway. Most of the windows are 17th century, but due to damage from bomb blasts in World War II, the glass is mostly modern. The fountain is by Butterfield (c.1885).

The porch was altered for Bishop Howley c.1814, whose arms can be seen in the vaulting. In 1929, the clock face was moved higher up to the bell tower, the upper window in the tower restored and the crenellation of the tower rebuilt. The bell, which sounds the hour, bears the legend "Henricus Compton 1676", the clock, dated 1770 was made by Edward Howard of Chelsea. Over a third of the Palace was leased to the Ecclesiastical Insurance Office in 1958. The bishop retained five principal rooms on the ground floor with a kitchen, dining room and bedrooms above. To achieve this, a large chimney was removed and dormer windows built.

Top right and left: Two heads in the medieval style added to the porch c.1814.

Bottom left: Postcard c.1920 showing Bishop Winnington-Ingram's car and the old chimney.

Bottom right: The gates have been dated by dendrochronology to 1495.

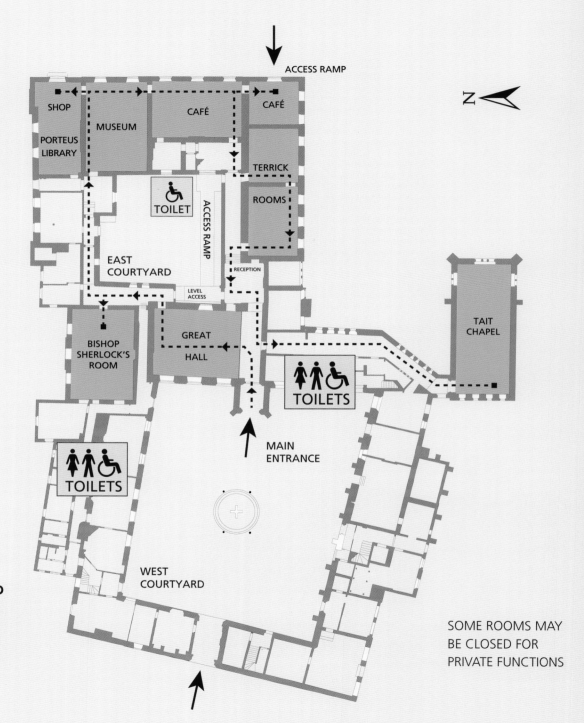

ACCESS RAMP

N

SHOP

MUSEUM

CAFÉ

CAFÉ

PORTEUS
LIBRARY

TERRICK

ROOMS

TOILET

ACCESS RAMP

EAST
COURTYARD

RECEPTION

LEVEL
ACCESS

TAIT
CHAPEL

BISHOP
SHERLOCK'S
ROOM

GREAT

HALL

TOILETS

TOILETS

MAIN
ENTRANCE

WEST
COURTYARD

**THE MUSEUM AND
HISTORIC ROOMS
ON THE GROUND
FLOOR ARE OPEN
TO THE PUBLIC**

SOME ROOMS MAY
BE CLOSED FOR
PRIVATE FUNCTIONS

The Great Hall

Top left: The oak timbers have been dated by dendrochronology to 1495.

Bottom left: The Catholic Bishop Bonner supposedly tortured Protestant prisoners here in 1558, from Foxe's Book of Martyrs.

Bottom right: The hall c.1899.

The oldest room in the Palace, the Great Hall, has been altered over the centuries as its function has changed. Unlike a family estate, each Bishop had to furnish the Palace himself, so the contents of the house have been dispersed.

The roof above the present ceiling dates to 1495, although there is a mention of an earlier hall in 1402. Queen Elizabeth I dined here in 1600 and 1602. The 1647 survey of the Palace describes a double-storey; "two great rooms over the hall with a little room on each side of them". These were removed in the 1750s when the present ceiling was inserted by Bishop Sherlock to make a lighter, more fashionable room.

The room was converted by Bishop Howley in 1814 into an unconsecrated chapel; the panelling, overmantel with its fine carving, and stained glass were moved across from the chapel built in 1766. All that remains of that glass are the earlier 17th century lozenges of different dioceses in the east window and four panels now in the Museum. When the present chapel was built in 1866, Bishop Tait restored the hall "to its original purpose", installing a screen brought from the Court of Arches, Doctors Commons, and adding the inscription over the fireplace. Older people still recall the wonderful children's parties held here by Bishop Winnington-Ingram in the 1930s.

Bishop Boner *burning the Hand of* Mr THOS TOMKINS, *to try his Resolution, over the Flame of a Wax Candle, in the Hall of that Tyrant's House, at Fulham in Middlesex, now the Seat of the present Bishop of London.*

Bishop Sherlock's Room

This room was the main focus of the 2006 restoration funded by the Heritage Lottery Fund, Hammersmith and Fulham Council and the Fulham Palace Trust.

Sherlock wrote in 1749, a year after becoming Bishop of London, "I find there is a very old bad house and I must repair a great deal of it, and I am afraid rebuild some part". Built about 1753 in the fashionable rococo style, by an unknown architect, different contemporary plans refer to this room as both a drawing room and dining room. By 1818 it had become a kitchen; in the 1960s the Ecclesiastical Insurance Office converted it to a computer room, inserting a false ceiling and dividing the room into four.

No image of the original room survives, so it has been reconstructed using archaeological evidence, paint analysis, comparison with similar rooms and principles of classical architecture. The fine plaster ceiling has been repaired; door openings, doorcases and panels on the walls reinstated, a new fireplace commissioned and an oak floor laid. The colour of the distemper on the walls is close to the original. The modern brass chandelier was donated by firms who worked on the restoration.

The paintings on display include Bishop Sherlock himself, George I, Henry VII and Field Marshal Wade. The three in matching frames were acquired by Bishop Tait for the Great Hall but were later displayed in different rooms by his successors.

Left: Thomas Sherlock c.1750 after van Loo, oil on canvas.

Right: The kitchen c.1895. Visitors were puzzled by a kitchen with such a richly decorated ceiling.

Bishop Howley's Dining Room (Museum)

This former dining room was part of the enfilade designed by the architect S P Cockerell for Bishop Howley in 1813 providing four communicating rooms along the east façade. Mrs Howley inherited money from her East India Merchant father, John Belli, which may have helped to pay for the extensive work, estimated at the time to cost £20,000. She told her husband's successor, Bishop Blomfield (1828-56) that they had 970 people to dine in 1827 both at Fulham and the town house in St James's Square.

"I dined at Fulham…the greatest part of the Palace is quite new - the rooms very magnificent in their dimensions - and superbly furnished… the dinner was completely French and I assure you that his Lordship lives in a very great style" (J W Whitaker 1820). In 1911 twelve or more guests daily would be sitting down to dinner in evening dress, waited on by a butler and two footmen. After the First World War meals became simpler, but still benefited from the fresh vegetables and fruit from the kitchen garden. "The Chaplain ordered the meals, he loved breakfast and the breakfasts were gorgeous…sausages, bacon, kidneys and scrambled eggs and delicious marmalade". Friday, however, brought fish three times a day! (Mrs Storey, Bishop Winnington-Ingram's great niece in 1992 recalling her visit in 1931).

Top left: The museum tells the story of the Palace.

Left: The Dining Room c.1899.

Right: Archibald Campbell Tait as Archbishop of Canterbury. Attributed to James Sant. Oil on canvas c.1880.

The Museum of Fulham Palace

In 1958 the room was converted for use as an office. In 1992 the Fulham Palace Trust restored the room and opened it as a museum interpreting the history of the site; its archaeology, architecture, garden and social history. The light green/grey colour on the walls and woodwork was recreated after traces of original paint were analysed, and can be seen throughout the rooms around the east courtyard. Note the uniform door cases designed by Cockerell which bring a sense of symmetry and order to an irregular building.

Fragment of tin-glazed plate: Dutch c.1686-1701, by Adrianus Kocx

Mitre: Embroidered damask. One of the first objects acquired by the Museum.

Panel of painted glass: Signed E. M Pearson 1771.

Mummified rat: Found in the roof of the west courtyard.

The paintings on display are part of the collection started by Bishop Porteus, added to by successive bishops and are now heirlooms of the Diocese of London. Amongst the four panels of stained glass (conserved by the Trust) is a rare example by Eglington Margaret Pearson who worked with her husband in the late 18th century. The magnificent cope and mitre were made for Bishop Winnington-Ingram c.1910, possibly by Watts and Co. The archaeological finds range from Neolithic pottery (3000 BC) to a mummified rat. The dolls' house has been furnished to show different period rooms. The model by Ben Taggart (scale 1:50) shows the Palace as it was in 1998, prior to the restoration project.

The Porteus Library

This room is called after Bishop Porteus (1787-1809) who made provision in his will for the building of a library to accommodate his collection of books and portraits of his predecessors. Porteus, a committed opponent of slavery, had 145 books and pamphlets on the subject. His portrait can be seen over the fireplace.

Until 1813 the Gothick chapel designed by Stiff Leadbetter for Bishop Terrick (1764-77) occupied this site. Porteus had a horror of being buried alive, so in accordance with his will his body was left for several days in the chapel to ensure that "return to life is naturally impossible". Porteus's estate could not provide sufficient funds for a new building so Bishop Howley's architect, Samuel Pepys Cockerell,

converted part of the chapel into a library in 1814. Note the handsome vaulted ceiling in the style of Soane, the original bookshelves and the jib door concealed by faux books leading out to a corridor.

Most of the glass in the Palace windows was destroyed in 1944. The painted glass still in situ shows the arms of Bishop Winnington-Ingram (1901-39); Bishop Bonner (1540-49; and 1553-59); Henry VIII; and the badge of the Bishop of London. From 1958 the library was used as an office. It was restored by the Fulham Palace Trust in 1992. The books have been lent or given to the Museum, as the Porteus Collection itself is on loan to the University of London.

The Drawing Room and Breakfast Room

These two rooms, now occupied by the Café, complete Cockerell's enfilade along the east front built in 1814-18. The unusual plaster frieze below the cornice is one of the few to survive in the Palace. The handsome neoclassical marble chimneypiece of c.1780 came from Appluldurcombe House on the Isle of Wight and was installed in 1952 at the suggestion of Seely and Paget, then architects to the Diocese of London. The crystal (cut-glass) twentieth century chandelier was left behind when the building was vacated.

The Drawing Room continued to be used as such until Bishop Stopford's retirement in 1973. Each bishop would bring his own furniture and might redecorate to his own (or his wife's) taste. In the 1930s tea was an informal meal, served here at 4.30pm. In 1938 Queen Mary was entertained to tea by Bishop Winnington-Ingram after a private screening of the 1912 silent film "From the Manger to the Cross".

Beyond the Drawing Room is a delightful double-aspect room. In 1766 this room formed the base of a Gothick tower and was used as a bedroom but by 1813 it had become the Breakfast Room. In 1897 Mrs Creighton chose it as her private room and breakfast was then taken in the dining room. Four years later Winnington-Ingram used it as his study. At Christmas the servants would file through one by one to receive their presents.

Bishop Terrick's Rooms

Top left: Richard Terrick (1764-77). His coat of arms can be seen over the entrance to the Great Hall.

Bottom left: The classical ceiling in the Drawing Room is one of only two to survive in the Palace.

Bottom right: The Chaplain's Study (as it was then known) 1929.

These two rooms, the "Terrick Rooms", formed part of the south façade designed for Bishop Terrick by Stiff Leadbetter in 1764-6. He provided a sequence of rooms on the ground floor which formed the fourth side of the east courtyard; a servant's bedroom in the base of the south-east tower (now part of the café), connecting with the bishop's bedchamber and beyond that a drawing room.

An 1813 plan shows this drawing room unchanged, but the bedchamber had become a dining room and the servant's room a breakfast room. Cockerell's 1814 alterations left the two "Terrick rooms" much as they were, although they were now designated the Bishop's Library and Chaplain's Library. Howley also commissioned Cockerell to remodel 32 St James's Square, the Bishop's town house acquired by Terrick in 1770. The town house was finally given up in 1920 and the Diocese was run from these two rooms until 1973. In the 1930s, the Bishop's Library included early Agatha Christie novels on its shelves, and visiting children could play table tennis there in the Bishop's absence.

There is fine carving on the door case, skirting and shutters. Although paint analysis revealed the first wall colour to be bright blue, the present shade was chosen to provide an appropriate background for a gallery. The woodwork around the windows, however, has been restored to its original and unusual blend of colours.

The Tait Chapel

The Chapel is reached by a corridor opposite the Great Hall. In 1857 Bishop Tait moved to Fulham with his family, but he found using the Great Hall as an unconsecrated Chapel was unsatisfactory; "my dear wife felt, as I did, that the ministrations for worship necessarily attaching to the chapel of the principal See House of so great a diocese required some more suitable arrangement. After much deliberation we determined to erect a new Chapel" (Tait 1879).

Above: Stained glass, angel from quatrefoil in east window by Ninian Comper 1953.
Below: The chapel today, watercolour.
Opposite: The Chapel in 1879.

This chapel is the fourth known at the Palace. Consecrated in 1867, and dedicated to the Blessed Trinity, it was designed by William Butterfield, at a cost of £1,869 and is arranged "choir-wise.", with the pews facing each other The polychrome brickwork (now overpainted) and inlaid stone were typical of his style, as are the brass altar cross and candlesticks set with moonstones on display in the Museum. The chapel plate dating back to 1653 is now in St Paul's Cathedral. The marble in the sanctuary was moved from the Great Hall and incorporated with Minton encaustic tiles. Fittings were donated; the organ by Robson was given by the Bishop's son Craufurd, and the archdeacons and rural deans of the Diocese contributed the glass in the west windows showing the four Evangelists by Clayton & Bell. By 1897 Bishop and Mrs Creighton displayed different taste, camouflaging the east wall with a curtain and placing their own altarpiece (of figures purchased at Oberammergau) in front. However Mrs Creighton declared "nothing can make that Chapel beautiful". A great-niece of Bishop Winnington-Ingram visited in 1931 and recalls two services a day, one before breakfast, the other at 10pm; "the boot-boy pumped the organ. We had to depend on the young lad pumping with a regular rhythm or else weird groaning sounds would come out with the hymns as the music wound down."

Following bomb damage in the Second World War the chapel was reorganised in the 1950s for Bishop Wand. The original glass mosaic reredos was moved to the west end. Brian Thomas and students from the Byam Shaw School of Drawing & Painting painted the murals (framed by a new plaster cornice) in 1953, deliberately obliterating Butterfield's decorative brickwork. Thomas's aim was "to present certain important dogmas and historical events of the Christian faith lucidly and memorably".

A plain ceiling was inserted below the original, the dark oak woodwork stripped and a new east window designed by Sir Ninian Comper at a cost of £1260 and paid for by war compensation. It shows the Risen Saviour delivering the command to St Peter "Feed my Sheep", flanked by portraits of Creighton and Wand, and the topmost angel depicts Bishop Wand's son who died in a mountaineering accident in 1934. The chapel, which seats seventy, is still consecrated.

Upstairs

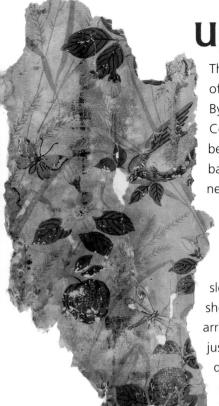

The upper floors of the Palace are offices and are not open to the public. By 1873 the rooms around the East Courtyard formed a sequence of bedrooms, dressing rooms and three bathrooms. Accommodation was needed for visiting clergy both from England and overseas, relatives, friends and ordination candidates. A future Bishop of Dover recalled his experience in the 1930s, "We all slept in dormitories in the attics… the sheets were not aired so all 60 of us arrived in our parishes with filthy colds just before Christmas". The servants' quarters were in the west courtyard and outbuildings. After the Second World War the west courtyard was converted into offices for organisations connected to the Church, such as the Historic Churches Preservation Trust.

Bishop Wand (1945-56), had been keen to give up Fulham Palace altogether, as being too large, inconvenient and too far from the centre of London. A major reorganisation of the private accommodation was undertaken in the 1950s for Bishop Montgomery Campbell. A small dining room with a kitchen alongside were made on the first floor. The wallpapers chosen by Jane Montgomery Campbell, the Bishop's daughter, were still in place in 2005 prior to restoration. Analysis during the restoration project (2005-6) revealed some of the original paint colours (which were reinstated where practicable) and scraps of early hand-blocked wallpaper.

Top left: Hand-blocked wallpaper c.1815. It contains at least 12 separate colours.

Bottom left: The upper floors, left empty since Bishop Stopford's retirement in 1973, had become derelict in places.

Bottom right: The bathroom fittings were all raised for Montgomery-Campbell as he was so tall.

The Gardens

The gardens at Fulham Palace are protected as an important historic landscape. Only 13 acres now remain of the original 36 which included the meadow now used for allotments. The surviving layout is mainly 19th century, with some 18th century landscaping, and includes many rare trees. The Protestant Bishop Grindal introduced the tamarisk to England on his return from exile in Switzerland in 1559. However, the most renowned gardening bishop was Henry Compton (1675-1713) who developed a famous collection of plants, both hardy and exotic. The estate was landscaped for Bishop Terrick in the 1760s during the rebuilding of the house when the formal enclosed gardens shown on John Rocque's map of 1741-6 were replaced with open lawns providing views to the river.

The grounds have always had several functions; providing food for the household, a beautiful garden for relaxation and a space for both recreation and hospitality. The celebrated garden parties were started by Bishop Tait's wife Catharine in the 1860s. Bishop Creighton (1896-1901) exhausted his guests by taking them for fast walks around the estate. His successor Bishop Winnington-Ingram, (1901-39), a keen sportsman, played tennis and hockey there. He opened up his house to convalescent children from the East End slums and allowed fetes in the grounds. After World War II the estate had to be run on more economical lines and the gardens went into a gradual decline.

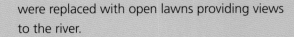

OUTDOOR MEN: "ARTHUR WINNINGTON INGRAM."

GARDEN PARTY AT FULHAM PALACE. July 893.

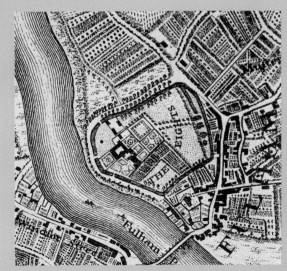

Noteworthy Trees at Fulham Palace

1. *Eucalyptus gunnii*
   Cider Gum

2. *Betula utilis*
   Himalayan Birch

3. *Tilia* 'Petiolaris'
   Silver Pendent
   Lime

4. *Acer davidii*
   Snakebark Maple

5. *Parrotia persica*
   Persian Ironwood

6. *Zelkova carpinifolia*
   Caucasian Elm

7. *Aesculus
   hipposcastanum*
   Horse Chestnut

8. *Fagus sylvatica*
   Beech

9. *Catalpa
   bignonioides*
   Indian Bean Tree

10. *Prunus avium*
    Wild Cherry

11. *Morus alba*
    White Mulberry

12. Bishops' Tree

13. *Robinia
    pseudoacacia*
    Locust Tree

14. *Quercus fastigiata*
    Fastigiate Oak

15. *Liriodendron
    tulipifera*
    Tulip Tree

16. *Magnolia
    grandiflora*
    Large flowered
    Magnolia

17. *Magnolia delavayi*
    Delavay's
    Magnolia

18. *Acer griseum*
    Paperbark Maple

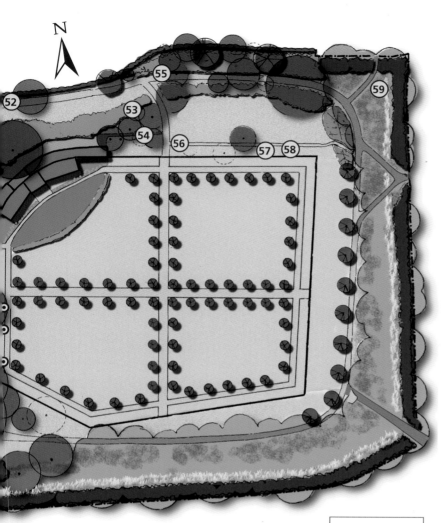

29. *Cryptomeria japonica*
Japanese Red Cedar

30. *Cercis siliquastrum*
Judas Tree

31. *Liriodendron tulipifera*
Tulip Tree

32. *Sequoiadendron giganteum*
Giant Sequoia

33. *Sorbus intermedia*
Swedish Whitebeam

34. *Ailanthus altissima*
Tree of Heaven

35. *Liquidambar styraciflua*
Sweetgum

36. *Cedrus atlantica*
Atlas Cedar

37. *Cedrus atlantica*
Atlas Cedar

38. *Arbutus unedo*
Strawberry Tree

39. *Cladrastis kentukea*
Yellow Wood

40. *Castanea sativa*
Sweet Chestnut

41. *Quercus cerris*
Turkey Oak

42. *Metasequoia glyptostroboides*
Dawn Redwood

43. *Gingko biloba*
Maidenhair Tree

44. *Quercus coccinea*
Scarlet Oak

45. *Parrotia persica*
Persian Ironwood

46. *Pinus ponderosa*
Western Yellow Pine

47. *Gleditsia triacanthos f. inermis*
Honey Locust

48. *Quercus ilex*
Evergreen Oak

49. *Fagus sylvatica var. heterophylla* 'Aspeniifolia'
Cut/Fern leaf Beech

50. *Koelreuteria paniculata*
Pride of India

51. *Quercus robur*
Common Oak

52. *Sequoia sempervirens*
Coast Redwood

53. *Nothofagus dombeyi*
Dombey's Southern Beech

54. *Pinus sylvestris*
Scots Pine

55. *Platanus x hispanica*
Plane

56. *Quercus castanifolia*
Chestnut Leafed Oak

57. *Quercus x hispanica* 'Fulhamensis'
Fulham Oak

58. *Paulownia tomentosa*
Foxglove Tree

59. *Ulmus procera*
English Elm

⊙ Bee Boles

19. *Quercus suber*
Cork Oak

20. *Prunus x subhlrtella* 'Autumnalis'
Winter Cherry

21. *Cedrus deodara*
Deodar Cedar

22. *Fagus sylvatica f. purpurea*
Copper Beech

23. *Catalpa bignonioides*
Indian Bean Tree

24. *Morus nigra*
Black Mulberry

25. *Malus hupehensis*
Hupeh Crab

26. *Acer triflorum*
Rough Barked Maple

27. *Halesia monticola*
Snowdrop Tree

28. *Juglans nigra*
Black Walnut

Botanising Bishops

Several of the Bishops were keen gardeners. Grapes were sent annually by Grindal to Elizabeth I: "the vines at Fulham were of that goodness and perfection beyond others that the grapes were very acceptable to the Queen" (Strype 1710). However in 1569 the grapes were sent late, in September, and the Bishop was accused of infecting the court with plague, as a servant of his had died at Fulham. Grindal wrote to explain that there was "none sick in my house"; the servant having died of other causes.

It was Henry Compton (1675-1713), however, who gave the Palace's gardens world significance. A serious student of botany, he was keen to import rare species. As Bishop of London, he was Head of the Church in the American colonies, and he sent a Reverend Bannister, himself an able botanist, to Virginia as a missionary in 1678. Banister sent seeds and cuttings in 1683 and 1688 which were grown at Fulham including the sweetgum and box elder.

During his 38 year residence Compton collected "a greater variety of hardy exotic trees and shrubs then had been seen in any garden in England" (Faulkner). His achievements were celebrated by fellow botanists such as Ray and Petiver. At his death his collection was dispersed, although some trees remained. His gardeners included John Rose, formerly employed by Charles II, and George London, who later ran the Brompton Park Nursery with Henry Wise.

Top right: The black walnut tree in Palace garden. Compton's specimen had a girth of over 17 feet in 1894.

Bottom right: Bishop Blomfield (1828-56) continued the gardening tradition, cherishing the rare specimens at the Palace.

Bottom left: Oak bench in the form of Bishop Compton.

Garden Tour

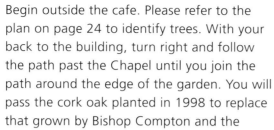

Begin outside the cafe. Please refer to the plan on page 24 to identify trees. With your back to the building, turn right and follow the path past the Chapel until you join the path around the edge of the garden. You will pass the cork oak planted in 1998 to replace that grown by Bishop Compton and the base of an 18th century sundial. The gnomon (the metal top) in the form of an R (perhaps for Richard Terrick) is in the Museum.

Turn left and walk ahead towards a large spreading tree. On your left is a fine specimen of copper beech. To the right is the woodland walk, following the line of the moat, and beyond the railings Bishop's Park and the Thames Path. A public right of way alongside the moat leading to the parish church of All Saints, known as the Bishop's Walk, had existed for centuries. Bishop Jackson granted the Bishop's Meadow to the vestry in 1883 and the park was opened in 1893. The large evergreen oak in front of you has been designated a Great Tree of London.

Follow the path around to the left alongside the red-brick wall past three bee boles (niches for straw bee hives). The wall and gateway are Tudor; the weathered coat of arms above is that of Bishop Fitzjames (1506-22). Enter the walled garden but please mind your head.

The Walled Garden

Top left: The wisteria pergola usually flowers from late-April to mid-May.

Bottom left: The knot garden in 2011 planted with perennials in red, yellow and blue for Bishop Blomfield's coat of arms.

Bottom right: The knot garden c.1899. The wisteria is visible trained on hoops. The glasshouse shown has since been demolished.

This two acre garden was first enclosed between 1764 and 1766 for Bishop Terrick. To your left is the vinery. Built by Weeks of Chelsea in the 1820s, it had been modified over the years but later became derelict. It was rebuilt by Alitex from 2010-12 during Phase Two of the Restoration Project. Following archaeological investigation it was reconstructed as closely to the original design as possible but for maintenance reasons was made from aluminium. The central section is open to the public.

In 1851, Samuel Hay, the Head Gardener, used the glasshouse as a vinery-pinery, raising two crops of grapes a year in spring and autumn including Black Hamburgh, as well as pineapples. An inventory of 1869 mentions "three mushroom beds in full bearing, a pine pit, a melon pit and 288 strawberry plants". When the Bishop was in his town house at St James's Square, vegetables, fruit and cream from Fulham would be sent there. The knot garden to your right formed by box hedges may have been laid out for Bishop Blomfield in the 1830s. By 1915 it was planted with irises and roses. In the 1980s Hammersmith and Fulham Council filled it with herbs. It was replanted in 2011 using the layout shown in early Ordnance Survey maps. The ancient wisteria (*Wisteria sinensis*) dates to at least the late 19th century.

Walk past the knot garden; turn right along the path and right again into the central avenue.

Top left: From: Gardens of Celebrities in and around London by Jessie MacGregor 1918.

Top right: Mrs Wand in the Vinery 1951.

Behind is the tower of All Saints Church.

The 1831 estate map shows a traditional walled garden layout with paths delineating the quarters and a path around the perimeter. Fruit trees were planted along the avenues and trained up the walls, while soft fruit and vegetables were grown in each of the sections.

Mr Cunningham, gardener to Bishop Tait in the 1860s, won prizes from the Royal Horticultural Society for his fruit including apricots, dessert apples (Fulham Pippin) and strawberries. Flowers were also needed for the house and flourished both along the borders of the paths and under cover. In 1911 there were seven gardeners at the Palace, but after the Second World War less produce was required for the smaller household and fewer gardeners were employed. Hammersmith and Fulham Council opened the garden to the public in 1974 and later used part of it as a tree nursery.

Turn right into the central avenue of apple trees and return to the entrance. The lines of fruit trees were replaced in 1990 using old varieties grown at East Malling. Recent archaeological investigation from has informed the reinstatement of the paths and the position of the vegetable beds, and the garden is gradually being brought back into productive use.

Top left: The bothies today.

Bottom left: The Indian Army praying for the recovery of King Edward VII in 1902. His Coronation had to be postponed.

Bottom right: Cows grazing in the Palace Meadow c.1895.

Leave the garden by the same gate and turn right. The bothies (the buildings behind the vinery) were used for tool sheds, a seed room, an apple room and living quarters. A junior gardener would have slept there to stoke the furnace heating the vinery. A James Errity is listed in the 1907 voters list as resident in the bothy. The derelict bothies were restored from 2010-12 and are now used by the Palace gardening staff and their team of volunteers. They are not open to the public.

Beyond the boundary hedge are the allotments. For centuries this area was known as the Warren (where rabbits were raised for food). By the 18th century it had been absorbed into the pleasure gardens, and became known as the Fulham Palace Meadow. In 1902 members of the Indian army camped there prior to Edward VII's coronation. In 1909 and 1910 it was the setting for two elaborate historical pageants with an estimated 4,000 performers and 6,000 spectators.

To the right is the route to All Saints Church and churchyard where ten Bishops of London are buried and the way out to Putney Bridge. The 1831 estate map shows an extra kitchen garden of over an acre here between the moat and the Palace Meadow. Visitors may prefer to continue to the left to see more of the garden or to return to the museum and café.

The Bishop of London

Top left: Richard Chartres, Bishop of London from 1995.

Bottom left: Edwin Sandys (Bishop of London 1570-77) with his wife Cecilia 1572.

Bottom right: William Warham, after Holbein. Oil on panel. As Bishop of London (1502-4) he was Keeper of the Great Seal.

The Bishop of London is the most senior bishop after the Archbishops of Canterbury and York. Mellitus was the first in 604 AD, and Bishop Chartres is the 132nd. He is responsible for the spiritual welfare of the people within the Diocese of London and ordains priests, conducts confirmations, preaches, and advises his clergy. The Diocese covers 277 square miles of Greater London north of the Thames and includes 479 churches and 150 church schools.

The role of the bishop has changed over time. In medieval England it was rare for people to be well educated so senior clergymen assisted with government or travelled abroad as ambassadors: in 1527 Bishop Tunstall accompanied Wolsey to France on a diplomatic mission. Today the Bishop of London is a familiar sight at national ceremonies. He has an official role in royal weddings and coronations, as well as commemorations such as Remembrance Sunday or state funerals.

The bishops of London were rich. In 1500 Fulham was one of about 24 manors owned in Middlesex and nearby counties. Church of England clergymen were free to marry from 1547 (apart from Mary I's reign) and could pass their wealth on to their families. Georgian bishops lived well: in 1828 Bishop Howley assured his successor, Blomfield, that although he would need to spend £8,000 a year, £13,000 would remain. In 1856 the Bishop of London's annual income was fixed at £10,000.

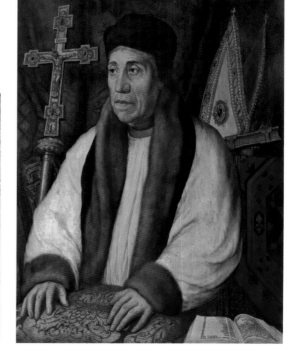

Meet the Bishops

**NICHOLAS RIDLEY
1550-53**
He was burned at the stake at Oxford, and became a Protestant Martyr.

SIMON SUDBURY 1361-75
He was killed during the Peasants' Revolt in 1381. His skull survives in St Gregory's Church Sudbury. This reconstruction of his head was made in 2011.

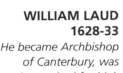

**WILLIAM LAUD
1628-33**
He became Archbishop of Canterbury, was impeached for high treason and executed in 1645.

**WILLIAM JUXON
1633-46**
He attended Charles I at his execution, and became Archbishop of Canterbury in 1660.

**FREDERICK
TEMPLE 1885-96**
Both he and his son, William, became Archbishop of Canterbury.

**ROBERT LOWTH
1778-87**
A renowned classical scholar, he wrote an English Grammar, which is still in print.

**ROBERT STOPFORD
1961-73**
The last Bishop of London to live at Fulham Palace.

**WILLIAM HOWLEY
1813-28**
He rebuilt much of Fulham Palace and officiated at the Coronations of both William IV and Queen Victoria.

604	Mellitus	1198	William of Sainte-Mère-Eglise	1597	Richard Bancroft
c.654	St Cedd	1221	Eustace of Fauconberg	1604	Richard Vaughan
666	Wini	1228	Roger Niger	1607	Thomas Ravis
c.675	St Eorconweald	1241	Fulk Basset	1610	George Abbot
693	Waldhere	1259	Henry of Wingham	1611	John King
c.705-16	Ingweald	1262	Henry of Sandwich	1621	George Montaigne
745	Ecgwulf	1273	John Chishull	1628	William Laud
c.766 - 772	Wigheah	1280	Richard Gravesend	1633	William Juxon
c.772 - 782	Eadbeorht	1304	Ralph Baldock	1646-60	*Bishops abolished under Oliver Cromwell*
c.787 - 789	Eadgar	1313	Gilbert Segrave		
c.789 - 793	Coenwealh	1317	Richard Newport	1660	Gilbert Sheldon
c.793 - 796	Eadbald	1318	Stephen Gravesend	1663	Humfrey Henchman
c.796 - 798	Heathubeorht	1338	Richard Bintworth	1675	Henry Compton
c.801 - 803	Osmund	1340	Ralph Stratford	1713	John Robinson
c.805 - 811	Æthelnoth	1354	Michael Northburgh	1723	Edmund Gibson
c.816 - 824	Ceolbeorht	1361	Simon Sudbury	1748	Thomas Sherlock
c.845 - 860	Deorwulf	1375	William Courtenay	1761	Thomas Hayter
c.860 - 898	Swithwulf	1381	Robert Braybrooke	1762	Richard Osbaldeston
c.860 - 898	Heahstan	1404	Roger Walden	1764	Richard Terrick
c.900	Wulfsige	1406	Nicholas Bubwith	1777	Robert Lowth
c.909 - 921	Æthelweard	1407	Richard Clifford	1787	Beilby Porteus
c.909 - 921	Ealhstan	1421	John Kempe	1809	John Randolph
c.909 - 921	Theodred	1425	William Gray	1813	William Howley
c.950	Beorhthelm	1431	Robert FitzHugh	1828	Charles James Blomfield
957	St Dunstan	1436	Robert Gilbert	1856	Archibald Campbell Tait
961	Ælfstan	1448	Thomas Kempe	1869	John Jackson
996	Wulfstan	1489	Richard Hill	1885	Frederick Temple
c.1002 - 1004	Ælfhun	1496	Thomas Savage	1897	Mandell Creighton
1014	Ælfwig	1502	William Warham	1901	Arthur Winnington-Ingram
1035	Ælfweard	1504	William Barons	1939	Geoffrey Fisher
1044	Robert of Jumièges	1506	Richard FitzJames	1945	William Wand
1051	William	1522	Cuthbert Tunstall	1956	Henry Montgomery Campbell
1075	Hugh D'Orival	1530	John Stokesley	1961	Robert Stopford
1085	Maurice	1539	Edmund Bonner *(1st term)*	1973	Gerald Ellison
1108	Richard de Belmeis (I)	1550	Nicholas Ridley	1981	Graham Leonard
1127	Gilbert the Universal	1553	Edmund Bonner *(2nd term)*	1991	David Hope
1141	Robert de Sigillo	1559	Edmund Grindal	1995	Richard Chartres
1152	Richard de Belmeis (II)	1570	Edwin Sandys		
1163	Gilbert Foliot	1577	John Aylmer		
1189	Richard FitzNeal	1594	Richard Fletcher		

Some Visitors

As the Bishop of London has always been important, both as a senior member of the clergy and often as the holder of a government post, such as Lord Privy Seal, it was natural that monarchs would visit him at his home. During Elizabeth I's visit to Bishop Bancroft in 1600, two thieves broke into the Palace and stole a silver salt (worth four pounds) belonging to her. Bishops were abolished after the English Civil War and Colonel Edmund Harvey, who had purchased the Manor for £7,612 in 1647, is supposed to have held a banquet for Oliver Cromwell at Fulham. Other visitors included George III and Queen Charlotte who came to breakfast in 1817.

held him to ransom; centuries later, a Suffragette who invaded the Palace through the windows of Bishop Winnington-Ingram's study had to be forcibly ejected by his chaplain. In the 20th century charity balls took place in the grounds, and the Palace is now a popular venue for weddings and parties.

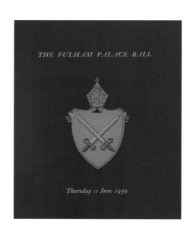

Bottom left: Richard Bancroft (1597-1604).

Top right: Princess Alexandra attended the Fulham Palace ball, held in 1959 in aid of Bishop Creighton House and St Etheldreda's Church.

Bottom right: Frontispiece to Creighton's Life of Queen Elizabeth *1896.*

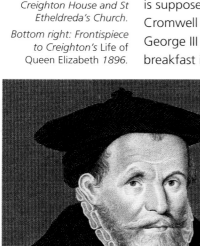

When the Palace was empty, the monarch had the right to use it. Henry VII suggested that the widowed Catherine of Aragon stay at Fulham in 1506 "for the sake of her health" in order to remove her from court and forestall her friendship with the future Henry VIII. Less welcome visitors included Geoffrey de Mandeville, who captured Robert de Sigillo, the then Bishop, in 1141 and

The Household

The early households were managed by the Bishop's steward while the Bishop would be assisted by his chaplains, but little is known about individual servants until the census was introduced in 1841. If the family was not in residence, a skeleton staff remained at the Palace, and other servants moved to the town house in St James's Square. The 1891 census lists 21 servants for Bishop Temple and his family. The butler, William Hebblethwaite was in charge of all the servants; the housekeeper, Mary Fletcher, was the next in rank, while at the bottom of the hierarchy were the scullery maid and the hall boy, Henry Pocock. Outside, the head gardener and bailiff, Albert Ballhatchet, managed the outdoor staff, including two gardeners and a stableman.

An insight into the household is given by a newspaper report of a burglary in 1893; the butler stated "they had a rare feed I can tell you...they ate everything, ham, pigeons and pigeon pies...they got at the wine too".

According to Mrs Creighton in 1897 they employed a butler, housekeeper, two footmen and a boy as well as "the necessary amount of housemaids and kitchenmaids", with 13 servants dining daily in the servants' hall. After each World War, the household contracted and fewer servants were employed. By 1961 Bishop Wand's household included a cook-housekeeper, driver and gardeners, as well as a secretary.

Left: John Turner, in 1931, aged 65, Head Gardener for over 20 years.
Middle: John Burley, Coachman, with his wife and their 8 children c.1917.
Top right: Elizabeth Maud Thorn, recorded as a housemaid in 1911, she left to work as a court dressmaker.

The Palace in Wartime

Top left: Bishop Winnington-Ingram was Chaplain to the London Rifle Brigade.

Bottom left: WAAFS outside the Gothick lodge 1944.

Bottom right: "A" ward May 1919.

At the outbreak of war in 1914, Bishop Winnington-Ingram proved an enthusiastic "recruiting sergeant". He spent ten days at the Western Front in 1915, staying with Field Marshal French, addressing troops at Ypres, and visiting the London Rifle Brigade. At home he faced pressure to release land for food production. Finally in 1918 the Council took possession of the Palace Meadow for allotments and the Palace itself was occupied by the Freemasons War Hospital Number Two, run by the Red Cross. The Porteus Library and Drawing Room became wards and the more mobile patients assisted in the garden. It closed in 1919.

In 1939 Bishop and Mrs Fisher moved to a London already at war. They slept on opposite sides of the Palace hoping that one of them would survive to raise the family. In September 1940 about two hundred bombed out people were allocated to the Palace for one night. Mrs Fisher wrote "all the carpets had to be fumigated" due to the "awful stale smell of crowded humanity". In 1944 a V2 bomb landed in the allotments. The Bishop had a miraculous escape as the ceiling of the main staircase fell in and doors were blown off their hinges. The ancient barn was so badly damaged that it was demolished in 1953. Barrage Balloon site 24 was based in the allotments staffed by a team of WAAFS.

THE LORD BISHOP OF LONDON
Chaplain to the London Rifle Brigade.

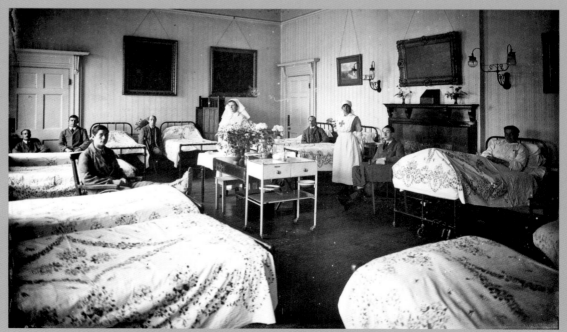

American Connections

There are many links between North America, Fulham Palace and the Bishops of London. Bishop Laud (1628-33) promoted the early settlements in Virginia and the Bishop of London continued to exercise spiritual jurisdiction over the colonies, licensing all clergymen and teachers until Independence in 1776. Samuel Seabury (later the first Bishop of the American Episcopal Church) was ordained Deacon and Priest at the old chapel at Fulham (now under the east lawn) in 1753.

Bishop Compton (1675-1713) imported many trees and plants from Virginia and grew them at Fulham, creating an important botanical collection. Amongst them was *Magnolia*

virginiana, the first to be grown in Europe. Bishop Porteus (1787-1809), the youngest of 19 children, was the son of Virginians who returned to England, settling in York. He was an active campaigner for the abolition of the slave trade, achieved in 1807 two years before his death.

Until 1897 the manuscript called in Britain "The Log of the Mayflower" was in the Library at Fulham Palace. It contains an account of the voyage of the Pilgrim Fathers and was given to the United States on April 29 1897. It is now in the Massachusetts State Library where it is known as the Bradford Manuscript.

St Margaret of Scotland (left) and Thomas a Becket, by American artist, Benjamin West. Oil on paper laid on canvas, these were designs for stained glass at Fonthill Abbey, home of William Beckford.

Henry Bishop of London

Henry Compton. Mezzotint c.1680-5.

Archaeology

Top left: Magnetic susceptibility survey by Archaeophysica in the walled garden in July 2009.

Bottom left: Fragments of carved stone found in the rockery.

Bottom right: Excavating the moat.

Historians formerly considered that Fulham was too low-lying and prone to flooding for early settlement, but it has now been established that the land was well-drained and ideal for occupation. The ford linking Fulham and Putney lay on an important strategic route, influencing the development of the settlements on both sides of the river. Excavations from 1972 to 1986 by the Fulham Archaeological Rescue Group revealed that the site was occupied during the Neolithic (4000-2500 BC), Iron Age (800BC to 43AD) and later Roman (3rd & 4th century AD) periods, and shed light on the development of the site.

Two programmes of archaeological work (2003-6 and 2009-12), associated with restoration of the palace and

its grounds, provided further evidence of the evolution of the historic landscape. Remains of a 13th-century timber bridge that crossed the moat were exposed when a section of the infilled moat was opened up.

Parch-marks that tantalisingly appear on the East Lawn every dry summer delineate the foundations of the medieval chapel just below the surface. Such observations, combined with archaeological investigations, help us to predict the character and survival of buried archaeological remains across the Scheduled Monument. Archaeology has a vital role to play in complementing documentary research to explain the development of this nationally important site and inform any physical intervention into the protected remains. As a multi-faceted discipline, it also offers exciting opportunities for learning and public engagement.